THE RECOVERY: COPING

ISBN Number: 978-0-578-67268-7

Power of Purpose Publishing
3355 Lenox Rd
Atlanta, Ga 30326

www.LoveAndLiveYourMessage.com

DEDICATION

First, I would like to give honor to God for allowing me to complete my first book. It's truly been a journey as well as a blessing. I would like to thank my loving family and friends for their support, as it is greatly appreciated. To those of you who are currently battling stressful situations I am in hopes that this book will bring you some closure. It is a daily process trying to come back from the things that have hurt us the most, but with determination it is possible.

THE RECOVERY: COPING

What does "to cope" mean? Take a few moments to define this term in your own words.

Do you have a meaning yet?

Coping is the ability to deal with difficult situations or having that capacity to do so. However, my question to you is, how many of us can truly say that we have "coped" with difficult situations? How many of us can say that we have gone through traumatic experiences that no longer affect us today?

Yes, there are people around us who seem to have surpassed all the hard times that they have had. There are people who have successfully worked through hurtful situations.

So, what about the rest of us who are constantly reminded of hurtful situations on a daily basis because we have not taken the time to work through them due to bottling everything up on the inside?

Well, I want to be as transparent as I possibly can with you. I am a person who has suffered and who is still suffering from hurt and pain that I just couldn't grasp enough to control and work out. My problem is the same as the next person, I just felt as if I didn't have the time to deal.

Growing up, my father wasn't in the home much. He was an alcoholic and a drug user. So, most times it was just me and my mother until my other siblings came into the picture. I watched my mother being abused physically, mentally, emotionally and verbally. Not only did I see abuse, but I was a victim of it as well.

We were constantly moving from place to place. And I always felt that I couldn't live a proper childhood. I was the one supporting my mother when my father wasn't around. I changed diapers, fed babies, dressed and bathed them too. I was put into a position to have to make adult decisions when I was only a child. Due to emotional and mental abuse, when it was time for me to start school, there was a disconnect. I didn't want to interact with the other children. I soon became a target of bullying. I was picked on for not having the best clothes, because of where I lived and even and because of my speech problem.

This lowered my self-esteem and I began to not like myself. I dreaded going to school and I only wanted to stay home because that's where I was most comfortable. I would have every excuse in the book as to why I couldn't go to school. I felt that my mother knew a lot of times I wasn't being truthful, but she allowed me to stay home because she needed me just as much as I needed her.

At the age of 9, I remember that not even a day after my youngest brother was brought home from the hospital, my father tried to kill us all due to an experience that he had from some drugs that he had taken. Shortly after my father was taken away, we became homeless. We moved to a small town called Plymouth and then to the town Roper shortly after.

I felt that a change in location would be better for me but bullying followed me while in middle school. When I got to high school, I can say that I wasn't bullied as much. Guys began to take interest in me but when I didn't give the response that they wanted; they would call me ugly and become very disrespectful. There was one guy who would call me ugly everyday out loud and of course this was embarrassing. By the time that I graduated my self-esteem was little to none.

I started college in August of 2009 and my mind wasn't in the right space. I ended up losing my financial aid due to my grades and attendance not being up to par. This sent me into a depressive state. I was seeing all my classmates going through college and succeeding while I was sitting at home. I picked up a job at Dollar General, which at the time filled any void that I felt due to being able to travel and get away with the job. But one day I realized this wasn't enough. When I decided to start dating it seemed that the men who wanted to pursue me all did me wrong. From lying to cheating, you name it; and truthfully all I wanted was to be loved. I made the decision at the age of 18 that it was time for a change, so I made a move and joined the ARMY. Though I had good times while in, I endured some very hard times as well.

I was sexually harassed and assaulted. I had an NCO who made a pass at me and due to not accepting her gesture she did everything she could to have me discharged out of the ARMY; from failing me on my fitness test to having another NCO claim that I was slandering her name. When I finally spoke up about the issues instead of getting help, I was just moved to a different unit.

My first marriage was while in the military. Things seemed to be ok prior to saying "I do". But shortly after, I was just being treated how I had been all my life. So, this was an ongoing cycle. In September of 2013 I was in a head on collision injuring my neck, back, and left rotator cuff, as well as having a concussion. The doctor prescribed me several narcotics. I began to use these medications to cover up all the hurt and anger that I was feeling, for a while it seemed to work. That is until I found out that I was pregnant with my first daughter. I discontinued the use of the pills, but I was so depressed and disconnected from the people and things around me that I couldn't function. My main problem was not being able to eat which jeopardized my health and the health of my little one. I was in and out of the hospital the entire pregnancy.

I remember being admitted into the hospital due to dehydration and elevated blood pressure readings. The doctor taking care of me ordered that I be given some meds to help with the nausea and excessive vomiting, but a side effect of this medication is that it made you drowsy. After finding out that this could be purchased at the local stores, I began to buy it just so that I could sleep my troubles and worries away. Towards the end of my pregnancy I felt it was best if I moved back home to have the support of my family when it came time to give birth to my daughter, since I was no longer with her father. This was hard for me. After having my baby girl in August of 2014, I had to leave not even a month later to return to duty, where I remained in a depressed state. So many nights I would cry myself to sleep. Going out amongst other people pretending that everything was ok was more draining than you could ever imagine.

I was able to go home and get my daughter in February of 2015. Going to get her made me so happy, but it caused a falling out between me and my parents which was very damaging. So now let's do a quick summary. My self-esteem and trust had been shattered. I had a long battle with depression. My emotional and mental state was unstable. And with all these ordeals, I didn't take the time to cope with any of them until recently.

It wasn't until recently that I chose to sit down and deal with my problems. It was time for me to be real with myself and it was time for a change. Not a temporary one, but a permanent one. I no longer wanted to feel sad and angry. I was tired of dealing with depression. I was tired of being triggered and exploding like a bomb when things or people reminded me of all those hurtful things that I endured in my life. And just like me I know there are others out there who are tired of holding onto situations that are hindering them. The best start is to talk about it!

Therefore, I felt a need to write this book. It's time to start your healing process. Let's work towards recovery together!

The Recovery: Coping

With this next portion of this book I want to go over some questions that I felt useful in my coping process. So that there is an understanding. But first always remember:

Philippians 4:13

13 I can do all things through Christ who strengthens me.

1. **What Is the Situation/Problem?**

   - Here I want you to explain the situation or the problem that occurred. Give vivid details. When explaining, ask yourself the following questions: When did this happen? Where did this take place? Who were the people involved? How long did the problem last?

2. **How do I feel about what happened?**

   - From experience, I come to find that our emotions play a major part with how we cope with different situations. Did the situation leave you feeling depressed, upset, angry, or sad? Did it leave you feeling fearful, regretful or

8

disgusted? Were there any positive emotions that you felt such as a feeling of relief, surprise, or unexpected joy?

3. **How did this situation affect me?**

   - This next question is very important, and I want you to take the time to really think about it before you answer. Has the situation made it hard for you to trust or let others in? Has it hindered you from conducting your everyday routine? Has it lowered your self-esteem? Do you have a wall up that you won't let down due to hurt? Has it changed your viewpoint towards anything? Did this situation break relationships? Did it build new ones? Has it changed how you view yourself?

4. **What was my role in the situation?**

   - Sometimes situations occur, and we contribute to the issue. Was there anything that you did that played a part in what happened. If so, what could you have done differently?

5. **Have you tried to cope with this situation in the past or have you tried to cover it up?**

- Many times, I have told myself that I was over something that happened when in reality I was just covering it up. Whether I decided to relocate or if I picked up a habit to keep my mind off of it, at the end of the day the problem still persisted. I was only covering up instead of actively trying to deal with my problems.

6. **What new approach can you take towards recovery?**

- After reviewing ways you have tried to cope or ways you've tried to cover up your problem, let's brainstorm our next steps towards working through it. If your way of coping was to remain silent, maybe talking and letting out your emotions could make things better. If you picked up a habit that takes your hurt and frustrations away temporarily, what can be done to make you feel better on a constant basis? I will be honest this part can be tricky, but YOU are worth figuring this out!

Now that we have gone through the questions and what to look for let's start to process.

What Is the Situation/Problem?

_____

_____

_____

_____

_____

_____

_____

_____

_____

_____

_____

_____

_____

_____

_____

_____

_____

_____

_____

_____

_____

How do I feel about what happened?

_____

_____

_____

_____

_____

_____

_____

_____

_____

_____

_____

_____

_____

_____

_____

_____

_____

_____

How did this situation affect me?

_____

_____

_____

_____

_____

_____

_____

_____

_____

_____

_____

_____

_____

_____

_____

_____

_____

_____

_____

_____

What was my role in the situation?

_____

_____

_____

_____

_____

_____

_____

_____

_____

_____

_____

_____

_____

_____

_____

_____

_____

_____

_____

_____

Have you tried to cope with this situation in the past or have you tried to cover it up?

_____

_____

_____

_____

_____

_____

_____

_____

_____

_____

_____

_____

_____

_____

_____

_____

_____

_____

_____

_____

What new approach can you take towards recovery?

_____

_____

_____

_____

_____

_____

_____

_____

_____

_____

_____

_____

_____

_____

_____

_____

_____

_____

What Is the Situation/Problem?

_____

_____

_____

_____

_____

_____

_____

_____

_____

_____

_____

_____

_____

_____

_____

_____

_____

_____

_____

_____

_____

_____

How do I feel about what happened?

_____

_____

_____

_____

_____

_____

_____

_____

_____

_____

_____

_____

_____

_____

_____

_____

_____

How did this situation affect me?

_____

_____

_____

_____

_____

_____

_____

_____

_____

_____

_____

_____

_____

_____

_____

_____

_____

_____

What was my role in the situation?

_____

_____

_____

_____

_____

_____

_____

_____

_____

_____

_____

_____

_____

_____

_____

_____

_____

_____

_____

Have you tried to cope with this situation in the past or have you tried to cover it up?

_____

_____

_____

_____

_____

_____

_____

_____

_____

_____

_____

_____

_____

_____

_____

_____

_____

_____

_____

_____

What new approach can you take towards recovery?

_____

_____

_____

_____

_____

_____

_____

_____

_____

_____

_____

_____

_____

_____

_____

_____

_____

_____

What Is the Situation/Problem?

_____

_____

_____

_____

_____

_____

_____

_____

_____

_____

_____

_____

_____

_____

_____

_____

_____

_____

_____

_____

_____

_____

_____

How do I feel about what happened?

_____

_____

_____

_____

_____

_____

_____

_____

_____

_____

_____

_____

_____

_____

_____

_____

_____

_____

_____

How did this situation affect me?

_____

_____

_____

_____

_____

_____

_____

_____

_____

_____

_____

_____

_____

_____

_____

_____

_____

_____

_____

_____

What was my role in the situation?

_____

_____

_____

_____

_____

_____

_____

_____

_____

_____

_____

_____

_____

_____

_____

_____

_____

_____

_____

_____

_____

Have you tried to cope with this situation in the past or have you tried to cover it up?

_____

_____

_____

_____

_____

_____

_____

_____

_____

_____

_____

_____

_____

_____

_____

_____

_____

_____

What new approach can you take towards recovery?

_____

_____

_____

_____

_____

_____

_____

_____

_____

_____

_____

_____

_____

_____

Many times we go through problems in life that seem too hard to handle. And though acting as if these situations never happened seems more ideal, it's best to work them out and not allow them to control who we are. So I encourage you to use this book as a guideline whenever a hard time arises.

Its time heal!
It's time to get your joy back!
It's time to recover!

Social Media:

Email: TheRecoveryTH@gmail.com
Instagram: The.Recovery.TH